ESCAPEGOAT

finding i'm human
trilogy series

ESCAPEGOAT

v.r. belmont

Escapegoat
Press

Escapegoat Press
a division of Escapegoat Productions
5073 Central Avenue #223 Bonita, CA 91908 - 0223

www.escapegoatpress.com
www.breethalamu.com

ISBN: 979-8-218-34742-0

Book cover idea by James Mills
Book cover illustration by Katarina N.
Illustrations by Victoria Rhodes

ATTENTION: READERS

This publication is designed to provide authoritative information in regard to the author's life experience. While the publisher and author have used their best efforts in preparing this book, they make no representations or warranties with respect to the accuracy or completeness of the contents of this book and specifically disclaim any implied warranties of merchantability for a particular purpose. The strategies contained herein may not be suitable for your situation. You should consult with your creator (God) and a professional (therapist) when appropriate. Neither the publisher nor the author shall be liable for any loss of profit or any other commercial damages, including but not limited to special, incidental, consequential, personal, or other damages.

DISCLAIMER

this book was written from a human's memory, which has a story to tell. but i have done my best to make it a truthful tell. i've changed names, dates and timelines so any character resemblance to real, living persons is just a coincidence.

-wink wink

i thank Jesus
because i was blessed all my life
a special thank you to my amazing
Uncle James and fabulous Auntie Tita
i love my Uncle James so so so so much
i couldn't have made the book without them
i have the best uncles in the entire world
thank you to
my Bishop Henderson and First Lady,
my loving Uncle Eric,
my beautiful Uncle Ian,
my Papa and Grammy
and Grandma

Baby Brother
you'll always be my blueberry muffin
i love you forever and ever, i hope to make you
all proud
i would not be here without my entire family
and loving community including my
sister, brother, God siblings
aunties, uncles, cousins
family friends, just friends
teachers and staff
doctors, babysitters, bus drivers
charities, food drives, shelters
and last but certainly not least
tax payers
while i'm at it
i might as well thank my mom and dad
i did not want to include them
but someone wanted me to add them on the list
and hopefully adding y'all to this list
will be my last and final
act of people pleasing that i do

now watch me escape.

contents

the sea goat........................*.11

the goat kid.......................*..43

a scapegoat...........*..............89

the browsing goat**...................117

escapegoat........................*..149

i remember writing my first breath
the most dangerous story written
i remember the war inside her womb
the most hateful space i've been in
i remember speaking my first words
acknowledging my experience
i remember my dark night's dragon
slaying in every direction

-i'm my mother's fetus

the sea goat

INT. HOSPITAL LABOR ROOM - DAY 1

In the coldest month during the year Atlanta
hosts the Summer Olympics and the birth of a
family's champion.

DISSOLVE TO:

EXT. MOTHERS WOMB - NIGHT

They pulled her head and out she came, and
proclaimed it's a girl.

BREE, the second born child to two humans,
long, bright eyed and cries until she's fed.

                         BREE
              the time where the bond
               is supposed to happen
             i wonder where i'll go first
              will they set me on a table
                 or the scale or her
             will they give me skin to skin
           or will they just sit me in dirt
              and say here to the ~~earth~~
                                      world

The nurse cradles BREE in her hands. A
Capricorn girl, not that ThAt means aNyThInG.

BREE

she slapped me on my butt
to welcome me here

i was afraid
she'd hit me again
so i did not inhale
instead she hit me harder
so i opened my mouth
and when she raised her hand
i pretended to cry
this was my first lesson in life

The MOTHER motions to hold her child. That was a
$39.35 bill.

BREE

what did i get myself into?

what was it that i
promised to endure?
i stare into my mothers eyes
trying to remember my
conversation with God

Her FATHER ran in late from traffic and he
prepared their transport to the car. The sun
was beginning to rise like the tears in his
chest. The MOTHER was obviously tired, furious,
annoyed, at her wits end, looking like who shot
John and forgot to kill him. Poor John,
everyone wants him dead. BREE looked just like
her FATHER, a 29 year old man :(

EXT. THE HOSPITAL - DAYBREAK

BREE only wanted to be drunk in love. No.
Smothered in it as they walked outside the
doors. Winter of 96.

                    BREE

          i told her to hold me close
          while my tears freezed cold
               i cried some more
          remembering His warning
                of a cold and
            broken-hearted woman
          i shiver thinking nothing
        can be colder than this wind

BREE knew to ask for her MOTHER too. Every
animal that is born always seems to know what
to do. The day they arrive, already knowing how
to survive.

BREE

the day after i was born
it was like she anointed me
with her bitterness when she cried
imagine needing attention as child
and hearing access denied
i cried
and cried
until i was by my grandmama side
sweet home california
the second year of my life

CUT TO: California

BREE wasn't the only one living in this condo
with Grandma. BREE had an older sister and her
baby brother was born right after who she named
BROTHER. The home had a slow leaking roof where
the corner of the attic wasn't good enough and
made her father leave farther someplace else.
Not only can a quarrelsome wife break a man
down, it's worse when it wasn't even a man to
begin with. But before he left them alone in
the "home", he'd been forewarned. The prophet
in Georgia stood and told him not to move to
California. He said "you and your wife will get
a divorce if you leave Georgia" and still they
went. DAD did what his wife wanted.

BREE

mother was sitting in the
saints memorial church pew
he slips her a letter
and then slips out of our lives
as i slip down into the water
now baptized
we're sitting in the back seat now
driving from church
i missed my friends
from the sunshine band already

i turn to my sister to stare at her
and i turn to my brother to
wipe his tear

he was a crybaby
like me too
i asked my mom
"where is dad"
she turned around to scream at us
and i could see
my prison sentence

INT. CALIFORNIA HOME - Day

Home, that's too strong of a word to use. It was located in the desert of Kern County California where the only comfort from the sun came from the skyscraper like palm trees.

                    BREE

            they were wide

        like the mane of the lions
        i'll eat in the days to come

BREE, was full for now. She had GRANDMA to walk her down the street, she had barbies tucked safely in a popcorn can, she had a lemon tree to shield her from the sun, she had 5-10 snail friends to play with. She's shocked at the lemon's bitterness, reminding her of her MOTHER and she cries whenever she has to go inside the house.

POLICE REPORT

BEGIN FLASHBACK: Long before BREE was born. An officer writes a report on his computer about a young woman reported missing.

a mother was once here
divorced from her husband
providing for her kid
and this wasn't her first time
running game
was she wrong for taking his money
was he wrong for wanting revenge
march 10, 1979, 23-years-old
this woman went to a club that night
location: 2 hours far from bakersfield, ca
3:00 a.m. the woman is escorted by friends to
her vehicle
and they stood and watched as she drove away the
woman did not go straight home
she decided to stop at a booth
and dial her ex-husband
he was home when he answered the phone
amidst the conversation the ex-husband
heard the phone booth door open
the woman screamed and yelled
helpless, scared
he could hear someone was hitting her
the ex husband also heard the woman say
"that guy came back,"
the phone booth door closed

END FLASHBACK 17 years later without a trace her kidnapper got away and found themself relocating near my PAPA place

INT. PAPA'S HOME - Day

PAPA's home always smelt right. BREE knew there was love and she could do no wrong. BREE knew she'd take trips to Disney and eat ice cream too. BREE knew Christmas would be magical and warm and beautiful.

                    BREE

          i thank God for all my have nots.
                like being aborted
               being in the system
                  being ran over
                  being touched
                  being starved
                   being burnt
                  being bought
            i watched each christmas pass
       with the hurt of the things i have not
                i try to be grateful
                 even if all i got
                     was her
                hand-me-down-hurt
                     all her
                hand-me-down-dirt
            and just enough to bury me in...

BREE really loves Christmas. But she couldn't understand that when you're a gift from God you're stuck here for good.

INT. PARKING LOT - Day

DAD let BREE sit in his work truck because her
MOM sometimes let him see them not all the time.
Usually I see him once or twice a year,
sometimes never. I guess as punishment or
because he hadn't begged hard enough to come
back into our lives. MOTHER swears he hit her…
like a narcissistic blow or was she talking fist
to chin who knows?
BREE thought she was cool because he drove an 18
wheeler and he bought her snacks from the store.
She remembers him vaguely watching her climb a
tree. She remembers sitting on the grass with
him. BREE never remembered him going, just that
he was gone.

BREE

where do they go?
when a "man" leaves his family
and does not raise his children
where do they go?
is there some far away land
where men just roam
i want to know
why do i have the strength to endure
what most fathers don't
if i had to live with her
why couldn't you?

BREE fought to remember her FATHER but 4 years
of memory was just enough to forgive someone.
She was angry because her FATHER should have at
least taught her to slay his dragon before
leaving her with it.

BREE'S ponytail

EXT. LOS ANGELES STREETS - DAY

GRANDMA got her grandbabies whatever they
wanted whenever they went to her yellow house.
GRANDMA and PAPA have been separated for a long
time but they both loved her equally. BREE's
Uncles and Aunties loved her too. She rode the
trolley with GRANDMA and they picked up egg
rolls downtown. They'd sit by the train tracks
and count the cars as they went by. 1, 2, 10
,15, 20, sometimes more than that. They'd walk
back to her yellow house and before turning
down the street they stopped by a man speaking
spanish. He was selling corn out his trunk,
still on the cob and wrapped in foil. BREE
never smacked her lips so hard before. It was
soooooo good. GRANDMA had a fat black cat, 5
black kids and 4 black grandbabies.

RECIPE

i dont know
but i do know
it aint good for ya no how

BREE

26

BREE loved food, especially Mexican food. She
loved GRANDMA'S house because she was full in
her belly and full in her heart. She was babysat
by her UNCLE who picked her up in the air and
let her build hot wheel sets. And he didn't tell
her "no, that's for boys". Back then toys were
just toys that required handy work. She was like
her GRANDPA in too many ways, good with her
hands that liked to build things up but tear
them down too. She loved cows and wanted to be
one so badly. She actually named her UNCLE 'COW'
as well, and has been calling him that ever
since. He lived with GRANDMA and he was the
coolest of them all. These were the best of
times.

BREE

some uncles are creeps
not my uncles
my uncles love me
they cover my eyes
during the bad parts in movies
they carry me on their shoulders
and tell me to reach the sky
they give me nicknames
and always ask if i'm hungry
they said i can be whatever i decided to be
i know my mama's uncles were creeps
i know there where bad things
that happened to kids
left in their company
i know my great-grandparents
raised them that way
in all their trauma
they was masters of war
and they'll succeed

my greatgrand papi was never right
when he came back from the fight
how was he to explain to his wife
that the white men in charge
hated him still, after fighting side by side
the part that's not in the movies
is what happened in the middle of the night
they'd lead them into a field
with sadistic in plight
it was the most humiliating thing
a white corporal could do to a privates life
with a gun to his head
they made him lay on the ground
and pull down his pants
and did things that could break
any good man's spirit
and knowing he'd never speak of this day again
he came back feeling even lesser than
and married a woman more
hateful than them
crazy right
how bad things
make you do bad things
and hurt your children
who hurt their children
who hurt their children
but in all their trauma
they was masters of war
and they'll succeed

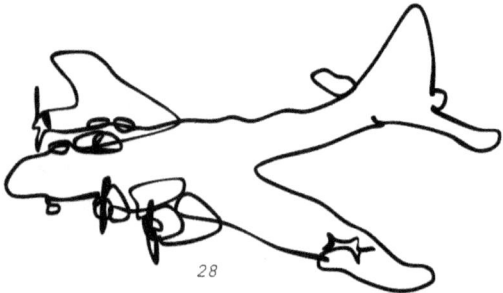

and 51 years later
was born BREE
i think about God and His hands in my life
i can now say
i was definitely prioritized

INT. GRANDMA'S HOUSE - DAY

One day BREE was with GRANDMA, she and her
siblings would play with the map. They'd point
to the countries to try and name them. GRANDMA
would scoop them ice cream of their own flavors.
Chocolate, vanilla, and strawberry. BREE held
her baby cousin at one point. She was smaller
than her. She gave her back to Auntie because it
was snack time.

                        BREE

        my brother was in line for some chips
                my sister was too
                and i was three
            my grandmama gave him one
             and gave her one too
                 and then me
        afterwards we had to get back in line
              and do it all over again
          my grandmama gave brother some
             and gave sister some too
    i came back with my brown paper bag and said
        imma need all mines at the same time
                please, thank you

BREE was different to say the least. She didn't
have time to play cute little games for children
unless it was MOTHER may i.

EXT. SOMEBODY ELSE'S HOME - NIGHT

One of the many men MOM knew, but not in that
way, BREE called him MR. R. BREE ran out of this
guy's house towards the street to see the
fireworks on the night of the 4th in July. She
had sparklers in her hands smiling and screaming
her head off too. It was soooo much fun. One
time he babysat them because just like GRANDMA,
BREE's MOM couldn't differend between the good
ones and bad men. That's every clinical
explanation you'll hear but if you asked BREE
her mother would have turned a blind eye to
anything if it meant getting money. BREE
remembers being in his bedroom on his bed in her
purple jacket. She remembered he had mirrors all
around either the roof or the wall and a little
dog.

                        BREE

      when you're young some things don't make sense
                  like the sourness of lemons
                   or the fear in your bones
                  like the sliminess of snails
                  and the crack of their shells
                  when you don't watch your step

but some days i'd be in daycare
my grandma would
pick me up thankfully
id walk backwards to the house
id run into poles and
shocked that i couldn't see them coming.
i begged her for water
one day i wouldn't stop asking
and so she said here
and handed me her glass bottle
"have some"
and it was gross
worse than bitter and it burned.
id sit and play with my friends
sally snail, claud snail, and slow poke
and stare up at the sky
wondering
why
me

wishing i was a princess
things women do to survive
they'd sacrifice they own kid
to keep themselves alive

If you asked my Uncle apparently none of this
would have happened if my DAD never left

INT. QUAILWOOD ELEMENTARY - DAY

BREE walks into her first grade class excited
mostly, school was one of the happiest places
on earth. You spent all day drawing, listening
to music and playing outside.

                    BREE

             during arts and craft
         the class' mom came in to volunteer

     BEGIN FLASHBACK: the day before we had career
                       day
           a real fireman came in to speak to us
       and gave us all firemen hats!END FLASHBACK

      she asked us if we remembered the emergency
                    number by heart
     she asked us if we knew our parent's numbers by
                       heart too
            she asked us what our address was
              and i could feel my heart race
        i remembered my mom said to never share that
                         part
               never tell anyone where we lived
             i kept making my gingerbread house
                  and ignored her request
              i should have gotten used to the
                 skipped beats in my chest
                     but i never did
                   the last thing i wanted
               was to endanger the family

                        32

INT. QUAILWOOD ELEMENTARY - NEXT DAY

BREE walks towards her centers inside the
classroom before the school day ends. First
there was reading, then there was art and then
building blocks.

BREE

savannah and miracle
were my best friends
miracle had blonde hair and bright blue eyes
and savannah looked identical to pocahontas
we were coloring one day like we always did
miracle said we were only allowed to color with
the pretty colors
she picked up the crayon container
and removed all the brown, black and gray
crayons
and set them aside, and everybody started to
color
i was shocked, i didn't know what to do
so i waited until they all finished and walked
away
i colored myself in all my landscapes i drew
brown for my face, black for my eye, brown for
my hands
gray for the skies
i threw them back where they were
hoping they wouldn't noticed they were used
i walked away whispering to myself
aren't i pretty too

BREE stands by the door inside the classroom
for the best part of the school day, lunch!

one day after recess i stayed to clean the
lunch tables
afterwards the cleaning crew got to visit the
principal's office
and pick out a jolly rancher or two
however there were plenty of days i walked
inside
with my head held high
acting like i cleaned that day
and took candy with my friends who didn't
clean either
life was simple and fun at once
it was routinely, not busy, i cried a lot
but not too much
and back then my sister liked me
and that was good enough
i swore to everybody we was twins
and they believed i was held back
a grade

There were many days BREE wished she was
adopted but she never was until adulthood. But
we're not telling that story. We're talking
about what happened way before then.

INT. CALIFORNIA HOME - NIGHT

We came home late one night and it was raining,
a rare sight to see in Cali. I don't remember
seeing the stars later that night. All three of
us made it in the house except my MOTHER. She
was trying to close the door. The door kept
bouncing open. Maybe he had tampered the locks
again. She gives it one last go. With failure in
her efforts she looks behind the door to see a
toad stuck in the henges, MR. R wasn't the only
one trying to get in. BREE was heartbroken
knowing the toad had died that night alone in
the dark, in the cold.

                    BREE

        that evening i had piano lessons
          and mom tutored another student
      he was sitting in front of the window writing.
        something i couldn't do well at the time
           then the entire window shattered.
                    behind me
                 lodged in the wall
                 was what done it.
              a triangle shape thing
          she called the cops and told them
                that guy was back
        he was stalking us again, tormenting us
                calling the phone
                 over and over.
               she forgot to add
            its another man i made prey,
          who gave away all his money
        to a woman who didn't' want him
             was she wrong for taking it
        was he wrong for wanting it back?

If you asked my Uncle apparently none of this
would have happened if FATHER never left.

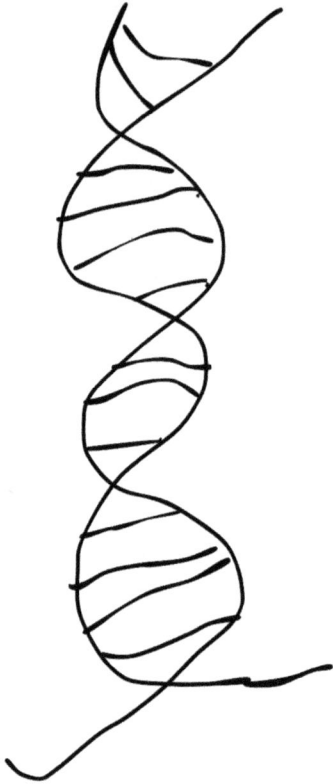

Summer '03 BREE was picked up by her MOTHER from
the babysitter's house. I miss this woman, her
name was SISTER EARLY. BREE'S summers were spent
riding bikes and falling down, eating playdoh
and memorizing the bible, sharing baths with her
brother and sister, playing with the
neighborhood kids and singing the fruit salad
song with the wiggles. Her brother and sister
run out the door with her to meet their mother.

BREE

i told my god siblings bye
and was surprised to see my mama's
cousin in the car
and even more surprised to know
sister early was coming too
i piled in the backseat with
my brother and sister
we sat in that car and made all the wrong turns
and watched as they all took their turns
first my mom drove
then my cousin
then sister early
they rotated once they got tired
my mom stopped for food and to use the restroom
it had been nearly 2 full days
we was in mississippi
my momma told me not to go far
because white men snatch up girls
out in the country
and the people hate us out here
they hate me and thay want me
at the same time
just like you mama
i thought

POLICE REPORT

BEGIN FLASHBACK: The private detective hands
BREE's mother a brown envelope the night of the
accident. As BREE skips over the shattered
glass window on her way to the carpet she hears
her mother gasp for air. Something in that
folder must have scared her. What didn't BREE
know?

BREE

mr. r's record of violence

he was a sad man
he bought everything
including love
the cops told my mom to get out of town
and it wasn't because they didn't want us here
but the guy they've been trying to take down
couldn't be bound
technicalities with this dna technology
apparently his dna was only in her corpse
and not on her clothes
and the dna they was trying to match
for a murder he admitted to
to help lower a sentence for a different
dispute
was lower than my mama iq
so we ran and kept on running
but of course i didn't know any of this news
i only knew summer was cut short this year
and that drive was longer than the usuge

7 years before BREE met Mr. R he tried to snatch
a teenage girl inside his car and opened fire
onto a couple sitting in theirs. 4 years before
meeting Mr. R he abused other women in a
domestic disputes. Before BREE met Mr. R he told
her mother he had night terrors and couldn't
sleep because of all the bad things he did in
his past. Her mom knew something was off about
him but she needed his money. So she told him
she wasn't married, though her divorce wasn't
final. She told him she wasn't getting back with
her husband and did the ole bate and switch once
she realized he wanted things more personal. And
when he finally popped the question she turned
him down, she said I'm thinking of getting back
with my ex, i just don't know where he is. She
said the divorce isn't even final because he
ain't signed the papers yet. He went to go
search for BREE'S FATHER, he asked BREE'S MOTHER
for all his money back and she told him no. So
here's a story about how MOTHER messed around
and found out. But let my Uncle tell it, none of
this would have happened if my FATHER hadn't
left town. END FLASHBACK

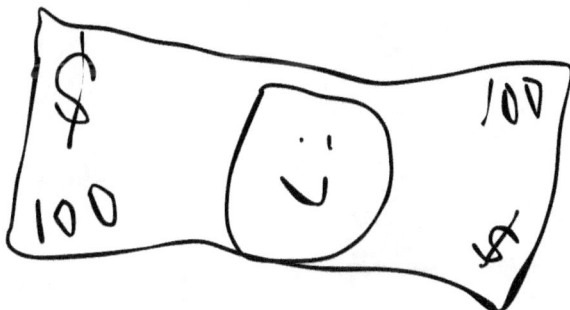

i'm the bloodline cleanser
the trouble maker
the eye opener
the whistleblower
that constant reminder
to go home and take a bath

-i'm my mother's kid

the goat kid

INT. ATLANTA, GA - NIGHT

BREE was in the backseat with her brother and
sister when her mom finally told them. They was
back were it all started.

                        BREE

                family always called
              they sometimes asked to see us
        but we only got to use the phone if mom said so
                on our way to school she said

                        MOTHER

                my name is _____ now
              that is what you'll tell people
              when they ask what my name is
                    you tell them _____
        i went and picked up y'all new papers too
              don't tell anybody where we live at
        don't talk to nobody and tell them our business
          kiki and them don't need to know all dat
              she be asking too many questions
                    in the first place
              you tell them hi on the phone
                and get off when you done
                  they don't need to know
              nothing bout what's over here
                don't say to nobody nothing
              don't be talking to yo daddy either
                  if he ever ask you anything
                    you tell him nothing
                  you don't got no friends
                  you don't need no friends

                          45

you have your sister and brother
play with them
you not going to nobody house
i don't know they mama
they daddy look like he like men
and they kid look like rats
been sucking on they head
you cant sleep over nobody house
don't ask me while we over there
don't ask me for nothing while we in the store
eat the food i give you
and be grateful
don't be in the fridge bothering
nothing you aint have permission to
don't go eatin up all the cereal
don't open up a new box
before the first one is done
don't go lookin for yo grandmama in the ice
cream
CAUSE SHE AIN'T IN THERE
you walk together on your way home
and don't stop for nothing
don't be leaving your coat at school
we ain't got nothing to give to them

keep the key inside your shirt
don't be swinging it around thinking you cool
don't nobody need to know you walking home from
school
we not doing gifts this year
we living with uncle reggie
and we staying here til we get our own place
we blessed to be here in the first place
there's a church we'll visit this weekend
and that's where we'll go every weekend
don't be up in these white people school acting
up

they don't like you already
they don't care if you pass
you better do all your work
and bring home all your books
u better not have a teacher
calling me while im at work
you better not be talking in yo class
or else when you get home you gonna get it
i want the house clean when i get back
and the kitchen swept before i get home from
work
and the garlic cut up and the chicken in the
sink
better not be up in these people's school
embarrassing me
you already cant trust these white folks
anyways
and they already looking for a reason for us to
get out
don't leave the house
dont go over nobody else house
don't open the door
dont go over to the door when it rings
don't nobody need to know you in the house by
yourself
have your shower before its dark
you ain't no white girl
don't be standing in the shower
and messin up your hair
and i ain't got no money to have it redone
you not going to the pool
i ain't got time for yo hair to be falling out
you not having a party
i ain't got money for dat
you ain't going on no field trip
i ain't got money for dat
you not having bbq at the school

you eat they free lunch
you not getting new clothes
i ain't got money for that
so don't ask me for nothing
dont talk to nobody bout nothing
and you better not start crying
cause aint nobody working harder than i am
and if you dont wanna listen
imma beat you and you can go live with yo broke
daddy
who aint got nothing, dumb, and talk stupid
or be in the homeless shelter
where they rape little girls
(pause, looks at son)
and boys
you need to say ya prayers
before you go to be
and be happy
for another day

For the people who don't know… that was our
version of the "birds and bees" talk every black
kid gets, so i thought.

BREE was in the second grade when they began
walking to their new school. MOM said listen to
your older sister and do as I say. Two very
complicated things to say to a kid that age.

MOM

walk down the street and go to class,
don't talk to no stranger,
don't wander of the path

BREE

she points to the sidewalk
and i started walking
sister turned back home
but i kept on going cause mom said so.
she wasn't about to get me into trouble.
i heard sister scream my name
BREE come back
but i said no
i gotta go where ma said go
but i didn't know she told sister to tell me
"come back"
i saw MOTHER step out the door and yell my name
and i felt a cold shiver
it felt like shame
i say to myself i hate my name
every part of it
i wish i was like that white kid
i saw last week
whose momma let him jump on the
roof of the car and throw fits
man i wish i could be like Joey
one of the bad kids

BREE scurried back to the doorstep to accept
what came. She made a mistake, an honest one
for real but her punishment.. you would have
thought she killed a man. Her mother was mean,
she was cruel. But ask MOTHER'S little brother,
none of this would have happened if her FATHER
never left.

BREE is starting to get sick, her and her
sister. Life is hard just like her time spent on
the toilet. Her sister had it worse because she
suffered more. They even put her to sleep and
she had her tonsils stolen from her. BREE didn't
know it then but being a middle child wasn't as
bad as having milk in the fridge.

LACTOSE INTOLERANCE

its good at first
a lil tarte
and truth be told
day old milk aint that bad
but 8 years is quite noticeable

spoiled
sour
acidic
fermented yuck

this was my experience nursing with mother
what she couldn't terminate at birth
she waited till afterwards
a huge mistake on her
trying to kill the heir
a girl none the less
the family's champion
not giving a care if i died with it
i asked her to wait
there's a better way to do this
little did i know
she never wanted me in the first place

BEGIN FLASHBACK: NIGHT

Before BREE was born.

THE LEMON ORCHARD

oxnard, ca between 2:00 and 3:30 a.m.
an old woman awakes at the sound of
a car engine idling in the lemon orchard
pop pop
she doesn't think anything of it
hopefully it was just the sound
of an engine backfiring

10:00 a.m. that very same morning
a man working in a lemon orchard
drove past a delicate hand, browned,
clearly visible underneath a water can
nearby were her shoes and clothing covered in
dirt
her car was left at the telephone booth
where the last person she talked to was her ex
husband
the cops arrive on site and identified the
victim

FLASHBACK ENDS

BREE hated pressing her hair more than her mother. Her hair fell out every year, it was brittle, broken and dry.

HOT COMB

she had cruel heat expel
like the summer sun
i was the oiled scalp
she touched me once
and that was enough

TO READER: writing this was taxing, detoxing and healing all together so here's the rest of my poems. Enjoy.

FLASH FORWARD: I found out in high school why we moved to Georgia. Mr. R was finally arrested and in prison around the same time. Yes everyone called our phone once it was in the news. Because he stayed close to old people we knew and got a job at our old church in CA. Yes I'll go visit him one day in prison, if he isn't already out, to know how our weekends really were spent with him in his house. No one went back to normal including MOTHER. If you watched me my whole life you'd think I was still on the run. I truly feel that they were meant for each other. All i know is opposites don't attract, but monsters do.

A DAILY ROUTINE

i woke up at 4 am
she yelled again and again
i cleaned the dirty house for two hours
even though it was just one spoon in the sink
i go back to bed to rest
she yells again and again
she says nobody in this house is more tired than
her
i stayed up until she went to bed
and then i went to bed
again another day comes
as if life is a gift that keeps giving
i get up realizing my lungs still worked
i peel my dead legs over
i scream at them to get up
i wait for her to yell but nothing came
i had time to take two breathes and so i took
three
i meet my siblings at the garage door
we gather empty gallons and headed down the
street
we made it to the neighbors house
and filled our bottles up
i reminded myself
this is only temporary
i stare at the sun
as it rose in the sky
i stopped to bury the fear
she gives me at night
i spoke to God
i said
teach me to fight

BREE went to school the next day. Middle School 2009.

ROLLING MY EYES

i remember my history teacher in middle school
i remember learning about slavery
obama had become president and
she told us that now none of us
had an excuse to fail in life
she told us anything was possible
she said we should be grateful
because other people in africa had it worse
she said we should be happy we don't have to
wake up at the crack of dawn to walk
get water from a well and bring it back home

this was the first time i saw the back of my
skull

BREE hated history class and their trashy
books. Honestly, who wrote these lies? She
didn't believe in Santa Clause nor slavery, it
couldn't be true, my people came from this
story written in glue. US history was an eye
opening experience, learning about a time that
BREE lived through. Not my people, not me ever,
said every black person alive. But more
importantly BREE couldn't fathom the thought
that more hateful people like her mother
existed in the world. Good thing she didn't
believe it because she wouldn't have been able
to get no sleep or get out of bed. She would
have quickly given up on life. Good thing she
ate an orange that morning and she swears it
kept her alive. Her head hits the pillow as she
hears a beautiful raspy voice sing about
pockets full of sunshine.

BREE remembering her mother. And how the world
around her praised the single ones and the odd
feeling of being a child of a narcissistic
parent.

SHE WAS A PUBLIC FIGURE

growing up she treated us well in public
she changed when the seasons did
and when you heard "cut"!
your clothes were drenched in blood
your wounds become real
real fast
so tell me
what do you do when you're a kid
and your mom's a superstar

WASH ME AGAIN

i am clean
intelligent and curious
inquisitive nature
with a constant desire
to explore and investigate

BREE remembering the times her MOTHER came home
from work.

PEEPING TOM

she should have named me tom
everyday i sat and watched
because i found it interesting
the way she changed the second
she got inside the house

she'd rip off her smile
wrinkle her brow
her mask would drop
to the floor with the
expectancy of 9 lives
i watched the devil get dressed

at age 7 i knew
this was not normal
at age 10 i thought
what an awful night show
at age 13 i said
get a room
at age 16
i prayed
i never get undressed

BREE remembering her "friend" her mom told her
she could not have.

ERIN

when i was in school i had a friend named erin
we weren't really friends and kindness kinda
broke off at the end
however i remember a conversation we had
the week of career day
my favorite day of the school year
erin asked me what i wanted to be when i grew up
excited to share a dream with her
i listed each talent interest and passion of
mine
architect
fashion designer
model
carpenter
interior designer
engineer
she stopped me with a stare
um you can only pick one
i was confused because i had ALREADY dreamed the
dream
she must not know what shes talking about
because its impossible to undream a good dream

BREE remembering her desire to be loved. BREE was the most sensitive child of the bunch of roses.

ORCHID CHILD

move me graciously
protect me from rain
but water me weekly EXACTLY at 8:00
face me east ever so gently
then sit back down mama
and watch me grow

BREE had to share everything growing up.

ICECREAM

*summertime days sometimes we'd go out for ice
cream after church
at our favorite spot called brusters as a treat
and people gawk at us eat
thinking back that was probably nasty to see
three kids licking one ice cream*

BREE on remembering her mother.

BLACK MAGIC

my mother or the witch she is
performed her first magic trick
we sat for mexican food
at our favorite spot
where one bowl made three burritos
i've seen magic before
living with a single black mother

BEGIN FLASHBACK BREE remembering her days in
elementary school. Mean girls mistaking her for
her sister and throwing leaves at her because of
jealousy. The leaves had red ants in them. Girls
ARE mean. So BREE spent most recesses alone by
herself or she'd play with the boys.

I WAS YOUR FLOWER CHILD

and this was my gift
i was good with my hands
i sat in fields of white clover
and braided them in my hair
this was that outside smell
this was that green streak on my knee
this was that georgia clay on me
that you said not to bring in your house

you hated that
dad came to the school
you hated the rumors
he is embarrassing you
you hated that
dad stopped by the house
and bought me flowers
that day you came home from work
and found them on the counter
you beat me for opening the door
or because you hated
that i did not hate him more
but we both know it was because they
weren't for you

i was your flower child
this was my gift
and my gift exposed you

BREE "here's your flowers MOTHER, now take them".

TRIBUTE

give them they flowers
while they alive
however
i give her flowers
in hopes she'll learn to become one

BREE remembering her mother's toxicity was
breathtaking.

MY JUGLONE JUICE

whenever i smiled
the juglone juice
i was ready to fly
then juglone juice

whenever i tried
the juglone juice
i sang too high
then juglone noose

i had to hide
the juglone juice
when the bees came by
then juglone truce

when i ate the rays
then juglone juice
straight from the tap
flowed my juglone booze

BREE remembering the games her mother played.

GAMEOVER

i lost when i forgot to say
mother may i

and took three steps forward
after hearing no you may not

she grabbed me by my hair and said
take three steps back

BREE remembering church life.

LOVE FROM MY MOTHER

this was my first introduction to God
which was why i never met him

BREE remembering her mother being overbearing.

MAMA BEAR

you come out when they're not there
i'd call you mama, but not like no bear
i need sleep in this house of hell
i've needed sleep haven't you tell?
i closed my eyes and prayed this prayer
die monster die there
that brought me peace, but i couldn't deny
it was darker than dark, it was darker was i
finally, sleep
and shocked to see
another monster,

me

BREE remembering her mothers death stare.

THE EASU COMPLEX

i would have mistaken your actions as friendly
but whenever she looked at me
i thought
cut me up why don't you

BREE remembering puberty. But also never sharing gossip, talking or doing girly things with her MOTHER. She hid everything like her period, as if instructed to by ancestors. As if masta was gonna come in anytime and snatch her up, take her to a barn to breed and bear children. BREE hid every dream, every wish , and good thing from her MOTHER. Planting it in poisonous ground, hoping it would grow and not get destroyed like her confidence and self esteem.

VIRGIN MARY

one day around age 12
i had a dream and
in order to see it to thru
i hid it from her
very well
too well
for when it came time to find it
i didn't know where to look

BREE remembering nothing. Her morning routine
was to clean and make up MOTHER'S bed, which she
didn't know was not normal til later on in life.
Sometimes you'll just be sitting with
people/friends talking and then they'll all stop
and stare wondering what you just said. Asking
"why doest your mom walk around naked in the
house" or " why do you need permission to go
into the kitchen for food". And they ask you to
repeat it hoping they heard you correct. You
find out you were abused when people don't laugh
at your jokes, when they say it's too dark or
look like they feel sad for you. You find out
you were abused when people say "yeah that's
weird" or "i been through that too". It makes
you wonder about life and what if it could have
been different and then you dream about a better
life that you have never been exposed to. You
dream about the white picket fence and green
grass beyond it.

BREE cleaned and organized her closet, usually
Tay cooked breakfast and Jay cleaned out the
trash and washed the bathtub and toilets. And
mother sat in bed on the phone everyday talkin'.

You know what I hear all the time people say to
me and excuse me if i'm breaking the 4th wall
writing code but I hear people say to me like
the reason why they believed my mother and not
me they say to me "well I know her, I don't
know you." They'll say "well I grew up with her
in school." So don't take things personally. A
lot of people honestly believe your abuser over
you simply due to their rapport. That's why it
was easier for them to just accept what she said
as truth. Because she called them every Sunday
and I they never knew.

OUTER BOOOTY

she beat us so bad
i was shocked to know
something other than God's beauty
could take my breath away

APRIL '08 BREE remembering her brother being born.

THE NEW ADDITION

oh boy
it's a boy
a baby boy
my baby brother
i'm gonna have a warm snuggle muffin baby
living in my home, this awful place
i'll keep him warm at night
while i listen to his
sweet snores of life happening
like warm snuggles and blueberry muffins
i get each morning before school

BREE remembering her baby bro.

BORN A FRIEND

brother you're brilliant
just as i thought you'd be
brother you are my blueberry muffin
warm spirited and self assured
your face turns brown when it's sunny
brother you are love
you're my favorite black person
brother you make news
and the coolest kid on the block
brother you forgive me
and make me stronger than i thought
brother we just click
and make jokes no one gets
brother you're my secret handshake
cause you make me feel like i belong
brother i am happier you are here
and i have your back
always
you're a much better friend than erin

My name is Victoria B. Rhodes. The B stands for
Blasphemy. Except I don't like Blasphemy. I
just like me and that's all.

A SINNERS PRAYER

one time a phone charger broke
and my mom was very very angry
these phone chargers were worth more than my
life
before walking into the store
she told us she'll pray to God
and He'll tell her who it was
she said she'll get the right one
i walked down the aisle so hungry
i walked by licking my lips
guessing the taste of every item
ma didnt want the food stamps
because we were better than that
i thought about stealing the snacks
i thought about ripping open the bag
and only taking a few out and putting it back
like i've seen people do before
i go to the nice white lady and asked
for another sample of chicken tenders
it was the biggest sample they had
then i go to the cold deli lady
and asked to sample some cheese
then i go to the sweet shop
and told them it was my birthday
for a free cookie
then i rushed to the attendant
and sampled their new recipe
when i remembered you could taste the grapes
prior to purchasing

i just remembered that i didn't want to steal
i didn't want God to punish me
i didn't want God to hurt me
He already tells my mom when to beat me
no sense in giving Him a reason to
she ended up beating us all
she said i'll beat all yall
to make sure i get the right one
she said to shut up and if i didn't
she'll try and break my neck
my mother always said
"you tell anybody what's going on in this house
and you'll be in a group home
and you better not think that they'll treat you
better than me
i'm your mother and little girls get raped in
there
that's what'll happen to you."
shoot i'd rather someone hate my body
than for someone to hate my soul
i would have taken that deal
to feel that feeling of whole
she said "when i tell you to do something, you
do it"
she told me "i better obey or else"
she told me when i got older "don't listen to me
you gonna run into the wrong person and they
really gonna show you"
then she'd laugh
she told me i better cry, because i deserved it
she told me " no one would ever love me more
than my mother"
she taught me what was love, she told me my
worth
she sold me my God

sometimes i think she forgets she was born
and once my age too
sometimes it feels as if she snuck her way onto
earth
and became something God forgot to remove
when we got home
before she beat us
we had to go get our own switch
and in the south there's a bunch of weeping
willow trees
all over our street
i opened the front door slowly and
placed my foot down the concrete step
wishing a car would just hit me
2 seconds later my foot's back on the curb and
i reached up to grab three branches for her
i gripped real tight to break them off
she puts them in braids
i don't usually speak to trees
but i apologized this time,
cause i did this every week
i went my way back home as i held them in my
hands
and used my sweat to pull off all the leaves
i watched them fall with one drop of pee
i let go the naked switch and handed them to
her
as my brother and sister watched me undress to
my underwear
i walked to the bed
when she said take those off too
i knew it wouldn't be long
because the small ones left visible scars
but i knew she didn't care
i knew it'd begin when i saw that grin

and then, i tried to run
but she grabbed me by my head
and slammed me on the ground
i got back up
cause to hell this witch
but i was too small too thin
all she had to do was sit on me
and i'd lose all wind
when it was over
i ran to the corner in my room
i wrapped my arms around my knees
i drew a pattern around the welts on my legs and
on my butt
i was careful not to lean on the wall
because i'd put pressure on the ones back there
too
i started to blow softly across the marks on my
arm
i rocked back and forth i cried for hours
until my sister came around the corner to offer
me dinner
and before i ate
i prayed the sinner's prayer

Abba Father who's not in heaven
hallowed be my chest
when will you come?
who is your son
that died for me to rest
that gave me this mother
that gift her a daughter
she tournaments to impress
who breaks her soul and eats it cold
and grins at every chance

and lead me not
to obey a book
she uses in her way
to excuse her hate
to speak my fate
to plan my days of pain
and forgive me Lord
that your lamb has gone
to walk a path unknown
come find me Jesus
tonight i runaway from home

God did not Love me i believed
and i had this pulsing deep deep cry
that vibrated my chest
i felt the blood pushing me
to go along with this game we play
where i hate everyday i live
where holding my baby brother
to my heart, made me apologize
i felt darkness surround me
and lick my wounds
like the devil cared for me
better than she ever could
in my soul, i could feel God no more
i knew he was real
just not real enough to fix my problems

i couldn't sleep at night
most times i'd cry
some days
i imagined taking a knife
and _____ it in her _____
9,000 times
finally my heart beat slowed

escapegoat

my eyes closed
cause in my dreams
my monster
couldn't get to me
i was finally at peace
i felt lesser exposed
after
tricking my body
in thinking
it was safe at home
and this is why
it dont trust me now

BREE was never able to "get with the program" no mater how hard she tried. Anytime she wanted to do something she always heard "why you trying to be on yo own program"!?

FAMILY ACT

the reason why i don't
get along with my siblings
isn't because
we don't get along
it's because, well
shoot if i knew shunning another sibling
got me in good with the parent
i'd do the same thing too
that meant less attention away from me
and more on you
we all did what we had to do
still i love my siblings through and through
besides they the only friends i got

BREE makes regrets.

SIBLINGS

i made them see the truth
and they hated me for it
i realized its best
for people to realize it
for themselves.
telling them to hurry up, will make them angry

BREE'S alarm clock woke her up for many things.

SET A REMINDER

to be sad everyday 7am-7pm

if i ever forgot
she'd remind me
i ain't got a dime
nor a pot to piss in
and a dime nor a pot to piss in
will be handed down to me or my siblings

i was reminded every day
i am not a dime because i have this face
and i ain't got a pot to piss in because
i have no window
i am simply me
i am supreme
i am bree

its five o'clock already

BREE wanted to be a cow growing up. But you already knew that. It has nothing to do with MOTHER calling her a heathen and heifer all the time.

DOMESTICATED

since i'm a cow today
and was one yesterday
i'll allow you to raise me as yours
and sale my milk
eat my meat

i'll be the cow for now
along with the grass it eats
and the twigs that hoist me up

i'll be the blood that rush to my head
the steak on your plate
the pressure i'll raise in your body
the fat that clogs your arteries

i'll be your cow today
like i was yesterday
i'll allow you to raise me
just remember i'm His kid
now say your grace
to God be the glory

BREE never heard girls will be girls. Because girls had harsher consequences for staying a girl too long.

Prodigal Daughter

i prayed to God
make me her son
black moms love their boys
and hate their daughters
God make me her son
so i can go a day without a shower
so i can dream about my father
so i can start a fight
and be lazy and be okay to be angry
and feel invisibly more
God make me her son
so i can make mistakes
after years of constant mistakes
and come back to open arms
no intent to care for her in her older days
no plans to leave my boys will be boys phase

so i can be given everything and amount to
nothing and
show no respect but have unlimited chances to
gain it

I shouldn't be feeling this low, and if you asked any of my Uncles they'll just say none of this would have happened if my FATHER never left.

every toxic person fuels
themself with something
being toxic benefits them
otherwise they'd be healthy

you besta hope they on drugs
and not on you

-its too late

a scapegoat

BREE remembering the time she wanted to be good. MOTHER had called everyone into her bedroom. She said "who be talkin to their FATHER?" TAY and JAY said "not me". BREE accidentally told her DAD what school she went to on the phone. MOTHER was very angry. She told them BREE talked too much, she pointed at BREE and told them she was a traitor to the family. SHE ACTUALLY LITERALLY USED THAT WORD LMFAO but on a serious note it crushed her. She begged saying "I will do better, let me try again, don't kick me out, I can be good I promise." My siblings never treated me the same again. I mean… BREE'S siblings never treated her the same again. Like when she was 15 and the visiting prophet came to their church. She called BREE to the front and said in front of everybody. "One day the world will know your face." Everybody started clapping and praising the Lord. BREE'S heart dropped to the floor and broke through to Hell, this was worse than receiving a compliment in front of her MOTHER. BREE couldn't believe this woman dared to rewrite her fate. BREE laughed; she thought all the prophets looked up the church members on facebook before arriving to preach. BREE thought all prophets asked around the church to find out more information prior to prophecy. This woman hadn't done enough research apparently, cause I can never show my face. I'm not allowed to have social media, besides they call me antisocial and besides my mama said my nose is too big. When BREE walked back to her seat she could feel a war begin to breed. When she reaches to grab for her armor she thinks to herself i aint no punk and continues on without it.

-self-right·eous greed

BREE knew she was being set up to fail by the
chocolate milk not johnny's appleseeds. She knew
her MOTHER would rather see her fail then be
successful without her.

I'LL PUT YOU ON A MILK CARTON

as an infant my milk came from
the sap of a walnut tree
which flowed booze i call the juglone breeze
it'd sweep you off your feet alright
and forget to catch you
so others can look and say
the apple doesn't fall far
from the tree

BREE knew her MOTHER to be angry everyday.

ANGER

when she would get upset
she would get really upset
then talk about it for twelve more weeks

BREE remembering the day she waved her white
flag.

WASHING MACHINE

each morning she'd wash me
in her washing machine
and i noticed there weren't
enough cycles that would make me
what she wanted me to be

i'd come out with soap in my eye
smelling like a citrus breeze
i'd beg her to stop
i told her i'd get back in
to repeat her trials

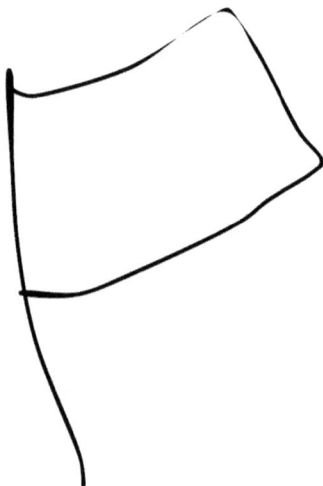

BREE loved going to the movies.

BLACK FEATURE FILM

you told me how if i kept it up
you'd try and take my life
but you only said what was said to you
i was sad because you told me my nose was too
big
but it's okay because you hated you too
you told me i was just like my father
and we all knew it wasn't a compliment
you told me how selfless you were
because you fed me food

if i had the guts i wouldn't have lived
all the times you promised me dead
i wished you did

INT. GEORGIA HOME - Day

Mornings were just that. The part of the day
where you experience deep sadness and the
disappearance of happiness called dreams. Where
i'm a superhero capturing villains hiding in
lemon trees.

BREE

i say to the rooster
wake me up in the morning
so can i hear my grandfather's words
cut through my citrus tree
wake me up in the morning
so i can feel my grandmother's hands
beat me til i pee
she goes outside
to watch if the sun will rise
so i whisper i pray i die
i pray the sky disappears
for the rooster to choke
i pray for peace
i pray, i hope
for the crescent shape of the moon
i pray to the wicked depth of the west
i prays for sleep.
i prays for help.
i smile as the sunsets
and she cries because
i have not broken yet
i am her daughter
a little jaguar
and in the jungle
from a motha

that's fowl

BREE grew up knowing she was raised by a woman who became the worst of both her parents. She's glad she didn't have her FATHER, he would have damaged her more and he was weird anyways. But let the games begin.

LETS PLAY A GAME

is normally what one says before you start to
play
not afterwards

BREE remembers being the middle child.

DiD I dO tHaT?

what happens when you're blamed for wrong
goings?
well the best revelations happen
i chose to do whatever i wanted
since i was gonna catch hell either way
this was the birth of me
this was the birth of BREE
she did what she pleased
begged for forgiveness never
i wasn't happy but i believed i was
my fears grew stronger than my will to live
i knew what i felt, desired, and thought was
unacceptable
but at least i got to be me in some form or
another
i was cooler than
danny phantom
half masked
half not
i was trying to be me
half triggered
half-cocked

BREE was broke like all the kids her age. She couldn't afford to replace the things she used.

IN HER HOUSE

you paid to breathe
every accident was a mediated thought
your no was yes
you had to turn your back to smile
the journey to womanhood was a threat
you chose to be in this world
your value was that of nothing guessed
and when you fail in ending your life
she's angry because
you didn't ask permission
like when you ate the last scoop
or drank the last juice

BREE was tired af.

OVERTHINKING @ 13

i thought every word everyone said to me was
true
i knew what my mother thought of me
i believed what she said to be true
i once heard a woman say i was beautiful
i thought she was complimenting me
i turned to say thank you

then i see my mothers face
my mother hated hearing compliments about me
i cringe
wondering why the woman couldn't just
compliment MOTHER instead of me now I'm really
gonna get it

so i tell people now
dont compliment me in front of her

BREE still tired af.

DESPERATE

bitter single mothers attract pedophiles
or sick men
abusive men
bad men
weird men
creeper men
i'm not saying having kids disqualifies you of a
life
im saying you need to question why this man
likes you
when the people you made don't
give af about you

BREE was tired af.

SHARECROPPERS

i watched my mother try
to destroy her own seeds

meaning me

so i proceeded to kill
the ones she planted

in thee

my lemon tree
removes her deeply noted

in me

and i brew it in tea
to spill pleasurably

BREE never liked counseling.

THERAPY IN THE BACK COMMUNITY

her therapy was a belt on my skin
my screams in the walls
my tears flowing into the sheets
it was my soul on the floor
and my pride behind door
her therapy was my spirit shattered
my bra tattered my panties on the floor
it was my apologies over and over and over and
more
her therapy was my confidence lowered
my head hanging low
which my shoulders followed
it was my skin flawed my smile gone
her therapy was my dreams devoured
my breath soured my voice quieter
it was my plea of guilty
her therapy was my self doubt
my reduced use of the word no
my desire to please
it was a broom, a spoon, a chair, a shoe,
a hand, the back of it too
anything nearby
it was an extension cord, a switch braided
it was her words which had words
those were worse
but thats how she healed

And if you asked my Uncle, none of this would
have happened if my FATHER never left.

BREE'S only memory of her mother was of
beatings, cooking or talking on the phone.

HOTWIRE ME PLEASE

she smiles
her voice is like liles
her words are wine
i think now is a good time
to tell her i need help
i have prom
i have sports
i have needs
i want wants
i looked over to see the line was open the whole
time
i didn't hear the phone ring
and now i feel stupid
thinking these good things would happen to me
she finishes her conversation
and told me the house needed to be cleaned
so i cleaned the house for 1,084,230,349th time
this year

BREE was tired all her life.

THINGS I WISHED I COULD TELL MY MOTHER

bro he's your son, not your husband
weird a__ h__

BREE loved going to church.

MY PASTOR WAS WORRIED

if a young woman like myself didn't stay in
church
id end up on a pole
dancing like a stripper
little did he know
my mother stripped me daily
of my happiness
of my dignity
of my light
who beat us like a bum
sometimes she'd be dead wrong
she'd never apologize
she'd tell us well
you probably did something i don't know about
she was wise
sometimes before she beat us
she'd say God told her who it was
she told us God knew who was bad
and that he spoke to her

what a snitch
obviously it was me
its been me everytime
but i was a good kid honestly
i thought bad thoughts
but only did what i was taught
i mean i did what i was told
i think i hate our God
telling her lies
lurking like a spy
watching my every move

i think i hate our God
having me live this life
then having to sing to Him
everyday in church
how He's a good good father
who don't keep you safe
whos always late
but also on time

forgive me Lordt

BREE'S eyes rolled once and never stopped.

PARENTAL ADVISORY

black mother's say
they child not acting right
reasoning is cause you not beatin 'em right

like who brags to other people on the phone
about how bad you beat your child over the
weekend
the south is weird af
for real
like hurry up and get thee out of here Satan

ask to speak to bree

BREE was confused.

SCAPEGOAT

i walked around the corner and accidently kicked
her glass of juice
i apologized and she yelled at me
she said i should be careful where i step

but when she walks around the corner and kicks
my glass by accident
she says i should not have had it in her way

i walk down the steps to wait by the car
i didn't want to be the reason we were late
she yells down you selfish kids come upstairs
and carry my purse
how dare you treat your mother this way
so next week i wait by the door
instead of waiting by the car ready
so when she comes out the room i can help
but this time she yells
why aren't you ready by the car
hurry up we're running late

what games she plays
there were always two sets of rules
one for me, one for her
i had to do what she say, not what she do
but what she say changes everyday
and i rather die than become this way

BEGIN FLASHBACK: Oh sweet Baby Jesus! BREE and the whole family took a break from church for about 2-3 months it felt like Heaven. If Heaven was on Earth.The best winter break ever!!!!! BREE wassssssss so happy she started shouting in the street. MAMA was big pregnant and once we finally went back to church. People were shocked to see us with a newborn. The mothers in the church came up to me and asked if it was mine! I was like what the world, no this my baby brother. I'm a Freshman in highschool! Boys don't speak to me unless they need pencil or paper. I remember the day he arrived. It was the last day of middle school. When I got home I went to the hospital to see him :)

HER EMOTIONAL VOMIT

the time i was a dog
my brother was 6 months old
i made sure i kept eating her vomit
so he can have somewhat of an
clean environment to call home

i can't believe i wrote this lol. dis nasty af honestly FLASHBACK EDNS.

BREE serves looks and american pie.

SWEET POTATO OR PUMPKIN

i designed my outfits growing up
i loved fashion
i loved myself so i thought
i loved making the hallway my show
and it bothered her
my walk, my shapeless hips my hairy legs
and skinny waist she'd tell me to eat more
she'd give me a slice of her humble pie
then make fun of me and in the same breath
brag to her friends bout my abilities
including the one where i predict deaths
confusing i know
one day she'll have her a piece and
i'm gonna stand back and watch her choke
cause i'm tired of having her back
lol i'm going to read this back one day,
wondering why i was so mad
then i'm going to remember the time
i told her it wasn't me
the times i begged, i pleaded
the hours i would cry
the time he said we dirtied his kitchen
when it was his other woman instead
still you beat me on my head
in front of him, i guess
to prove your loyalty
i promised myself i'd never be that way
that dedicated to a man, thats sick
the time my blueberry muffin
couldn't tie his shoe fast enough
and he beat him bad

he was only 4 and you stood and watched
the time i stood up to stop him
and said you can't beat him
for something you aint teach him to do
then you yelled at me, hurt me
bust me with a chandelier
instead of protecting your own child
from an angry mean man
you told me i wasn't going to ruin this for you
like i'd be a deciding factor in your
relationship
all the times you told me to go into the room
and give him massages because he was in pain
the time you told him i was good
i mean he did have a TV
he had a big house, in a good neighborhood
he had a lot of money and i knew he could
change our lives
no more eating small meals, no more lights out,
no more bird baths, no more star gazing,
no more open windows to let out the heat,
no more food pantries, no more practicing the
cello in the dark,
no more cold showers, no more grilling in the
backyard,
no more homework by candle night, no more
staying at a different house every night, no
more searching for turtles, no more stealing
neighbor's water, no more dreaming of food,
no more running out of pads, no more hair
jacked up,
no more making my own clothes, no more asking
for money,
no more going without, he had enough
for no more praying to God

112

so i rubbed his back and i massaged his feet
i did what i had to do
obviously
i think men know
which girls they can have
which mother would believe
and which mother would laugh
i think men know
how much they can take
which women wont stand
which women load blanks

in order to get things done
i think the devil knew
when he take one woman
he take her children too

Because she was a 12 year old man who needed to
provide for her family. But let my Uncle tell
it, none of this would have happened if my
FATHER never left.

how can i help you?
just looking for a way out
and wondering if being in a cult
was only for white people like skiing
and money

-browsing goat

browsing goat

This was the time BREE went looking for answers
and found out.

SMILE UGLY GIRL

my mama called me ugly
she said my nose to
big not to smile
"so smile"
she would say
and that's the story of how it got so big
cause i practiced everyday in the mirror to
one day look good
she say my skin looked jacked up too
she hated me like she hated
cheap shoes
and i thought i was ugly too
i look too much like my FATHER
but it was okay
i never grew up wanting
pretty, i never wanted anything extra
cause i knew it would make my mother hate me more
i worked harder to be uglier, smaller, quieter
last thing i wanted to do was offend
her, make her think i want her man,
make her think i think i'm better than,
make her think i'm being fast,
make her think i be kissing boys,
make her think i think i have a choice

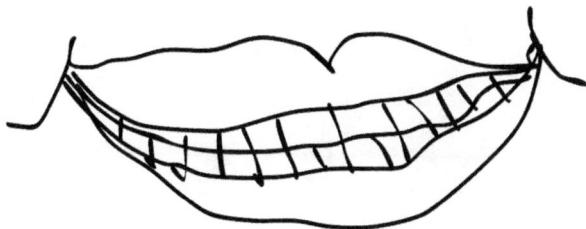

BREE had good dreams too.

THE GOOD GARDENER

water me honey
and every other day
set me beside the window
as i gather more sunny
tonight we'll all be sweet
sharing our flowing honey
as one big happy family
this never happened lmfaooooooooooooooooooo
but i'm still searching…

Some people help out of kindness and some people
help so they can look good and be bad. The worst
thing you can do is owe your MOTHER something.

HOSPITAL BED

if i was lying on the doctors table
and was drained of all blood
don't you dare volunteer
i wouldn't want anymore of you in me
let me go
be with God

BREE couldn't do anything right in her house.
She breathed razor blades and drank monomer.

MOUNT EVEREST

life's not fun
when breathing becomes a sport
i remember thinking
find higher ground
find higher ground
as she walked through the door

quietly as i stepped
wishing to be ignored
thinking i was invisible
like this egg shelled floor

everyday she came home angry
i knew for sure
i was gonna get it
i wished she'd wrap it up nice
least pretend you're giving me a hug
before blackening my pride

BREE never really talked growing up, middle school, high school. She was quite. Too quiet some might say.

SOFT SPOKEN

i once heard a woman say
i'm soft spoken
i whispered
no i'm not
in a monotone voice
because i wasn't living life to the fullest
and she heard it

i remember thinking
she wasn't loud enough

How come people never get my name right?

ITS RHODES NOT ROSE

if i had a flower for every time
my name was pronounced rose
i'd be red
like the blood from my veins
i'd be as sweet as my dreams
and as beautiful as they
imagined me to be

BREE had dreams every night, she knew things and
didn't know why. She saw things in people that
were obvious to her but blind to others. She
didn't know why she was born like this. She
hardly dare talk to anyone about it. She smiles
when you first greet her but usually she already
knew too much as you walked towards her. Some
might say it's because of trauma, she says that
it only made it stronger.

TELL ME ABOUT YOUR GIFT FROM GOD

i've walked past people before
knowing their story without being told
it's the kind of stuff you'd normally wait
for someone to open up about
the kind of information you save
for the 4th and 6th date
the things you whisper in a prayer closet
or write down on paper then burn in the fire

so yeah
it's uncomfortable
Knowing they deepest desires
seeing they broken wrist
and dying hearts
i could see the worst in people

i prayed to God, please take it back

BREE wanted justice for the crimes committed against her.

STATUE OF LIBERTY

i stood as a beaken
and threw my torch into the ocean
i wanted to go my own way
and try it without His light

DO NOT try this at home
this i can't condone
going without His grace
moving at your own pace
i don't recommend paving your own path
thinking your introduction to God
was your introduction to God

GRACE

He gave me grace
and she gave me hate
i did not deserve
like the life i lived
but safe from certain death
she put clothes on my back
that was beaten of life
with shoes on my feet
that shorten my stride
He gave me grace
which is why she made sure i ate
and had a bed without a home
and adjusted my sight
to run blindfold
He gave me grace and
grace gave me things i did not deserve
but my God, if you asked my uncle
none of this would have ever happened if my
FATHER never left

MERCY

Lord have mercy
i pray
least, He gives me His grace
Lord have mercy
i'd pray
or least give me your grace AND mercy

still, He gives me grace

JUSTICE

i hope grace meets justice
i hope she gets what she deserves
cause grace gave me hate i didn't deserve
i hope grace meets justice
oh
and God
have. no. mercy.

FLASHBACK STARTED when BREE wrote the title
actually. But to conclude Mr. R the reason why
his arrest took forever was because they didn't
give him a proper trial, there was some kind of
error. Originally the DNA was thrown out so they
had to come up with another way to submit DNA
for a fair trial.

DO YOU KNOW ME, DO YOU KNOW ME NOT

when shown photographs of his murder
he claimed he never met her
he claimed he never knew her
he refused dna and was arrested
they set up a camera
and interviewed him
they told him his dna was found in her body
again he said he didn't
he never met her
he never buried her
her never killed her
he never took her from k street
(pause)
the cop looked up and said
we never said where she was
taken from
(pause)
yall tryin set me up he says

FLASHBACK ENDS

Everytime BREE thought of her MOTHER she
cringed, anytime someone nearby raised their
hand too fast, too high she'd flinch. Everytime
she was told he was coming over she put on some
clothes, those shorts were too short, and the
top was too low. It's humid in summer, and black
men are getting shorter. Why do you care about
them more than your daughter… asked BREE.

JUST WEIRD MAN

as a girl your mother being jealous of you
is just as weird as your father being attracted
to you
black girls don't need to be beaten into
submission
i was an intelligent being
i wanted to be a builder
i mean
i wanted to be like Jesus
after church a lady pulled me outside the coat
closet
she asked me what i wanted to be
i told her a carpenter
i didn't know you was listening
you grabbed me aside and said
don't ever tell anyone that again
(repeats in a mocking tone)
"you wanna be a carpenter"
you're a girl

BREE

that's when i told everybody
i wanted to be a model
anytime i ran outside
you say you think i'm a boy
i just like nature
i like the birds singing to me
i like staring out the window
pretending im a deer
i dream of love
i dream in fear i'll never find it
i dream of running away
and finding a place with
an endless fountain of youth
to dip your sorry a__ in
you didn't know
i liked the sun on my face
i didn't care we ain't had running water
i didn't care we didn't have food
i only wanted you to be nice
tell me i'm pretty
hug me
ask me how my life is
be gentle to my hair
kiss my check
say you're proud of me
i liked walking in heels
and wearing strawberries on my lips
dripping peaches on my clothes
eating all the watermelon
and drying my fingers from peeling oranges
i ate my meals in one gulp
i was just young
but somehow also an adult
who wanted to make mistakes

not be told who to hate
like my father or family in california
or the gay people at school
i wanted to make friends
and who care if he wore a purse
i wanted freedom
like those shopping carts at walmart
why'd you give me to the wolves?
throw me out of the tree
tell me to hunt
after hand pulling my teeth
i was born in the dead of winter
i had good strong hands
i could have pulled you out of your sorrow
i was strong enough
i was our family's champion
i dreamed of slaying dragons
i dreamt i won every time
i dreamed you was mine
i dreamed i could be yours
i had good strong hands
stronger than my fathers
i could have healed your heart
all you had to do was be kind,
and not tear us apart

BREE prays, "rain down on me and take away the flames beating in my chest. I want to smile this week without the smell of lingering death."

DEW IN THE MORNING

Lord i want my conditions to change
where my experiences
no longer satisfies her need
i wish i did not cry where
my tears watered her greed
i wish i did not smile
where my laughter strengthened her punch
i want my legs to really be as long
as people thought they were

so i can run away and tell someone

can you see a
broken heart? or
two people
speaking?

BREE wanted something other than this.

ANNOYING

the most difficult part of growing up
was explaining your abuse as
your mom not liking you

and hearing that all parents
do what is in your best interest
knowing she was not

and hearing everybody makes mistakes
knowing she benefits

and hearing she loves you
she loves you
she loves you
she loves you
she loves you
she loves you
she loves you
she loves you
she loves you
she loves you
she loves you
she loves you
she loves you
she loves you
she loves you
she loves you
she loves you
she loves you
she loves you
she loves you
knowing she does not

this world weird af
since im already getting shunned
from the family for writing this book
let me continue.
she trash talk about all you
if she could sale you for
a million bucks she would
but don't worry cause she meant well
there's no handbook on how to be a good
sister, a daughter, a cousin, a niece, a friend
she doing the best she can

BREE

all i asked from her
was to be human
and this is why
when i ate chicken
i peeled off the skin
i tried hard
to kill the
monster within

BREE found a mask she wore for years and years
to come. Because being herself came with more
consequences than before.

POKER FACE

my healing process includes
writing your obituary
and a side prayer to the
parent i always dreamt of
and acceptance that
what lives today are
the deck of cards you handed me
sometimes i still stare
into my hands
hoping they'd slap me straight
and change my expression
to greaten my grace
make me appreciate my fate
and the days of pain
make me hate my ways
of hate
make me eat my plate
of love grains
and to pretend to understand
there won't be justice
and to learn that broken people
break people
just like hurt people hurt people
boi if i had a doolla
for every time
like i know now
but i wish i understood then
that if a person doesn't have love within
it's legally impossible for them
to give you something they literally do not have
LIKE THEY LITERALLY DO NOT HAVE IT IN THEM
they can't give you love because it does not
exist in them

they can't give you something not in their
realm.
IT'S NOT THERE
STOP
LOOKING FOR IT
IT'S NOT THERE
like the truth in these textbooks
like the program in your mind
how i look down on my peers
like the food fights they had
i called them ungrateful
i say they despise me
i say they beneath me
like i feel im better than
like how i made reasons to have no friends
i race to be raced
like mind tricks and spice
but i was just like them guys
how i tied my shoes to walk on grass
how i clean my water to drink
as i drive pass a tree
how my medicine keeps my sick
as i heat up my food
and keep my body from using it
i wasn't as special as i thought i was
everybody's going through something

BREE felt aloner than lone. Like lunch hour at
Arabia Mountain High. Like the time she ran up
to her sister to ask to sit with her and her
friends. She turned her back on her and said no.
So BREE ate lunch in the teachers lounge the
whole semester alone. She had no friends unlike
her siblings. She was aloner than lone. She was
empty. Like her stomach, like her MOTHER. But
most days when the family was hungry they went
to a friend's place to eat, when the water was
off they went to friends places to shower, or
after softball practice she took one at school.
She liked days like these when the power shut
off cause someone was selected to finish the ice
cream. We would grab the grill from the garage
and cook all the meat. And have grilled fish and
veggies. BREE always wanted chips, treats and
candy but MOTHER never bought those things. But
the times they ate, it was always healthier than
most. BREE drew her first building, a home with
solar power and two wells of water. She wished
her family never had to go without. Never had to
be evicted again and again, never have to be
begging again or staying with family friends and
taking people water down the street. During the
summer months BREE looked up all the days
restaurants give away free food. She designed
cow costumes for all her siblings so once Cow
Appreciation day came around they could get free
food from her favorite place. BREE didn't hate
the shelters, just the time they lived in. She
wanted her extended family around, she kinda
hated the South sometimes. Like the narrative
they sold about black kids and the white man's
hold on our lives.

They say this why we don't succeed because of
the bad black images on tv. But when you can't
listen to secular music, don't have cable or a
phone or technology and grew up in a box
praising the Lordt, patching your clothes,
staring into the clouds, and climbing trees you
see things differently. I always thought to
myself why don't they stop watching it then. If
it's gonna have them feeling that way. The only
time I felt I couldn't succeed was by the person
who birthed me. The beauty commercials and
magazines didn't make me feel unseen, my mother
was the first person to call me ugly. I wanted
to be many things like a carpenter and
architect, a designer and artist and I never
needed to see one to believe that I could be.
But more days than I could count I wanted to be
more blacker than black. I wanted to think like
all the others so I could join their pack and
their moaning and groaning to our God. After
spending all this time in Atlanta people still
ask me where I'm from. They know I haven't been
out much, that I have no fun. It's hard to talk
to the girls at my school when you haven't seen
the last episode or have the latest phone. It's
hard talking to the girls at my school because I
didn't know how to compliment a friend, grow my
hair, uplift with gifts, judgeless, blow kisses,
lend a helping hand, stop a bully, count on them
or share my food. However I did manage to meet
Abby and Charles. The best singer in the world
and the smartest guy I knew. But they thought I
was weird too and still do.

BREE loved a lot of things about her life like
the time her family visited from Cali, or the
times they visited them.

MEETING UNCLE JAMES

omg cali family!!! in da house!
was the best
whenever people visited the house
MOTHER was the nicest
the phone bill wasn't always paid so
we didn't know they was coming
it was just like Christmas
arriving in the middle of the night
touching they faces
felt better than life
i saw them black babies
for the first time in forever
i'm the second oldest of all my cousins
i like the responsibility i felt in they
presence
i like being the boss
and telling them the rules
i like when they call me by my middle name
BREE
but nowadays it's BREETHALAMU
it sounds like love
it sounds like peace
whenever i hear my family
shout BREE
i feel safe.
i feel free.
i hear the laughter they got
deep in they belly

i see they happy
i see they eat
they smell like love
they smell like leaves
like right after spring
a forever breeze
they was scared of the drive
deep in these country ass trees
so i tell them all i knew about my evergreens
one thing i loved about the south was the
school
even now i can name every tree
i can name all the animals
and the birds and what they eat
i homeschooled these westerns
like i was both adam and eve
they talk a lot and loud like bees
and they darker than honey
they dark like my dreams
they look like they met Jesus
like he kissed them on they cheek
they look favored and flavored
this made me cry in my sleep
i hate my goodbyes
cause the sun always leaves
after hugs after kisses
after california leave
i hate we not there
i hate to believe.
i wanted to go
i hate that i hate
that i hate
she said no
i met my Auntie new man
they say his name James
shoot i know mama is mad
hearing this news

cause on my father side
that's what they called
my daddy's dad too
til this day my mama
swear that's why Auntie
wanted this man
in spite of her failed
marriage with my father
the name james
apparently is famous
but caused problems
in this family
like when my uncle
called his brother
and asked him for the family name
my daddy had two daughters
so he told his brother yes
and my mama
ain't like that uncle ever since
plus when my daddy left home
uncle shack him up too
the name james
made my mama mad
like when she calls
my brother name
she pronounce it
just like my dad

i say hi to my new Uncle
i didn't really care, i thought
what he bring me from spain,
or europe or india
or brazil or anywhere
Auntie always
gives us gifts
and you're no different dear
when i close my eyes something
better appear
my new Uncle was quite like me
so i gave him a hug
then went to jump on my cousins
in the play area
basically my brother's room
i didn't know what to do
so i showed them our book
collection my Grammy got for us
and i showed them my cello
my music teacher gifted me
i let them touch my new jewelry
box Auntie sent from afghanistan
and i showed them my room
and all the things that i made
and i showed them my bratz
my grandpa bought for my birthday
i told them we got fred hammond
and mary mary
they said we dont wanna listen to dat
i told them nothing else was allowed

if i had a dollar for everytime
i heard this one
i'd buy my happiness
and sale it for free

-hurting BREE

escapegoat

BREE'S nda.

BY CANDLELIGHT

this little light of mine
i'm gonna let it shine
while holding it underneath the living room
curtains
burning them down so everyone can see
what's actually going on in here
somedays, i know i shouldn't say this,
but some days i was ready to walk through the
gates of hell
for every night i went to bed angry
i was already holding the door open for him
to wreak havoc in my lif

BREE loves writing poetry.

BREE

what i believe
poetic justice to simply be
is legal entitlement

BREE lost her stuff, her MOTHER lost herself

BREE

when we lost our house
my mother was mad
she thought she should be getting more help
from her family from her dad
but papa too old
to be still raising your ass
when grammy said no
that mad her more mad than befo
once she didn't make the bills
we had left the house and
put everything in the storage unit
she cried more over that chair
then when i told her
i fell, im hungry, i need care
when we couldn't afford the storage they
auctioned everything we owned off
all the memories, all the pictures
all our stuff
i wonder who where
my old clothes
i wonder who stares at baby me
if my pictures are in the trash
or the internet
or the street
at least i have my cello
and my backpack
i got's me
and as long as i
don't lose my sanity
im good with that
but mama took it hard
she loved stuff
more than she loved the Lord

This is when BREE knew it was time to go.
Everything annoyed her like certain sounds and
smells.

I WISH SHE'D SHUT UP

she'd complain day in day out
driving to and from
rain or shine
nothing made her happy
I MEAN NOTHING MADE HER HAPPY
not the milky way up high
however i
liked the night sky
i perch my head back
counting stars
and then i hear my mother
who speaks in numbers
she just go on and on and on

HE SAID, SHE SAID

there are certain events
that i can't guarantee
on this piece of paper
like my terrors at night
or her actions towards me
i would never kill for pleasure
but to end a living nightmare
that's a conversation i talk to God about
you'd have to go through
what i went through to begin to understand
what it's like being your mother's sick relief
what it's like when your own mind betrays you
it's good to take care of your body
because it'll take care of you
and make sure you forget
the worst thing that's happened to you

A DATE WITH IRONY

you brought me into this world
i want to take you out
these thoughts will bring you peace
but take you further from God
but know it's okay to be good
and just walk away
(from the situation not God)

JOSEPH

i was once gifted
a sugarcoat and
she destroyed it
i picked up the coat
i plucked the strings
to floss my gums
and still this day they pulse
i trusted them
they trusted gold
and prayed my death
and when i spoke to God
and heard him cry
i knew there was nothing
sweet about this day
yet still my teeth decayed
from her juglone juice
from my time down in the ditch
where i ate the lions within
and questioned my religion

SURVIVAL TACTICS

apparently a woman raising children alone
in survival mode
is not allowed to be held accountable
for her actions or life choices
so i say to all women live die ruin lives
as long as you a mother
you won't have to apologize

ANCIENT

you had ancient thangs to deal with
suitcases that ain't been unpacked since 1906
stories never told
praying to find out
everything that happened was bestowed to you
because someone decided not to do
what they was supposed to
you had to pray
to unbind from covenants
and finally breaking away
generations of
raids
maids
rape
sickness
poverty
pride
suicide
anger
and pain
so as you can imagine
i ain't wanna come to age
when i was handed the torch
days will come
where you'll want to toss
the thang into the ocean okay

OLYMPIC GAMES

passing the torch
had a whole nother meaning in my family
it meant it was your turn to fight
my battles
your battles
her battles
his battles
i guess
this is what comes from a lineage of silence
you deal with unfinished combat
a goliath dressed russian doll
debt rolled into one ball
speaking of which

DEAR GOLIATH

i got dressed that day
i volunteered as a tribute

the gate my mother paved for me
i ran towards
and chopped the head off it's being
i went back for round two
i killed it's wife
i tortured it's children
whose bodies i laid down to rest
these are the garments that
i'll save for my daughter
stained with the blood from their necks
so to show that
what i kill
WILL NEVER
resurrect.

BREE loved to see her DAD most times before
senior year of high school. Her family had to
move out of the homeshelter called transitional
housing and move into a roach infested two
bedroom bungalow where the neighborhood kids
stole our bikes.

MY EGO

whenever i think to share stuff mama do
my dad tells me all the time
"nOw YoU NnoW wHaT I HaD tO Go tHrOuGh wiTh Yo
MaMa"
like what kind of excuse... this sorry man
he think i'm about to feel sorry for him.
you're talking to a girl who endured
what scared you
i didn't have the luxury of walking out on the
family
there wasn't anywhere i could go to escape to
someone please check my stamina
there's no way i'm stronger than a man
this was the day i heard its heart beat
i started seeing a lot of women do this too
brag about the amount of pain
they could endure the longest
brag that they can do more than a man
better than a man
further than a man
faster than a man
badder than a man
safer than a man
greater than a man

i
dont
need
no
man
i said to him

because i am one

INNER VOWELS

i swear i'll never become like her
as long as there
is breath in the air
i swear
i swear
i'll never become like her
as long as i dare
until i leave here
i swear
i swear
i'll never become like her
and with my words
i sign my own death certificate

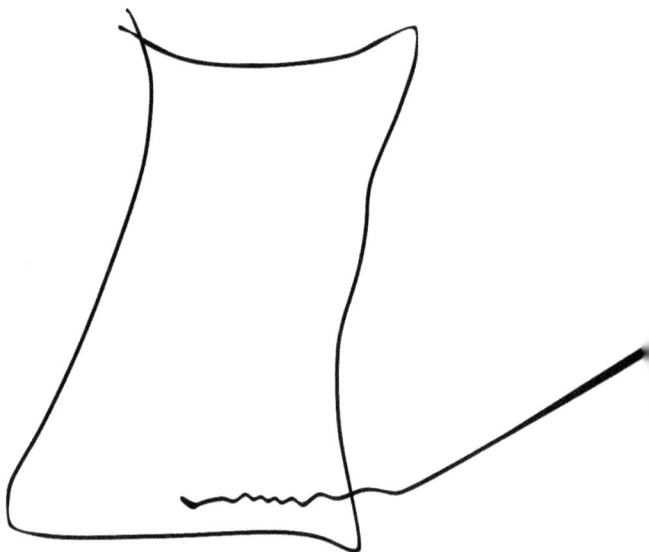

FEAR

i obeyed her due to fear
i went to church due to fear
good thing about that is, it wears off
bad thing about that is, it wears off

AFFIRM ME PLEASE

tell me i'm right
tell me i'm not crazy
tell me you believe me
even though you weren't around when i fell
just say you heard me hit the ground
then tell me to brush myself off and get back
up

LOVE

my mother loved me because i told myself she
did
i know this not because she's told me
i know this not because of something she did
i only know based off what i've said
if i can make myself believe something so bazar
then...
i know i am made for greatness
i know this because i said it
i'm no lesser than
no other man
spite what others think
i great
i am meek

ANCIENT ANGER

i learned the egg came before the chicken
i realized i've been mad at the wrong person
what happened to me was so ancient
it happened to my mother's mother's mother
it comes from a saying heard often
of what goes on in this house stays in this
house
it comes from being her stress reliever
a literal punching bag
i learned that it did not keep us safe
i realized it made me sick each day
what happened to me was so ancient
i'm sure it happened to you too

BREE

you'll always suffer twice
once from the what you tell yourself
and twice from your reality
you can get sick from just
telling yourself a bad story
and you can heal from just
writing a better one

NURSING HABITS

just about everything i did was coerced
if i knew making my own choices
would have still gotten me food
i would have said ouch mama
i would have given you the truth

MATH CLASS

the only thing that added up
in my life

HEALTH CLASS

the best text i ever read
was the one i wrote myself
at some point you gotta smile
and tell yourself you're beautiful
i spent too much time hating my face
i probably offended God
but he'd have to value my opinion
which i've learned he does not

HISTORY CLASS

whoever wrote these textbooks
need therapy

THE BLACK CURRICULUM

yOuR mOthEr GaVe bIrTh tO yOu
they always say
i wanna tell my story
that people will believe
how can i do this?
a black mother is more respected than God
i wanna tell someone a brutal
and honest story of my childhood upbringing
i wanna make conversations surrounding
the humanity of everyone's first relationship
around everyone's first superhero, their mother
i watched her fly i protected her love
i didn't tell anyone, i believed i deserved it
i thought i was doing things right
but i did my job so well now whenever i speak
people can't believe what i have said
how could everything change by this day
your mother is great your mother gave birth to
you
everytime i open my mouth im reminded of
the worst day of my life
so now i can't trust a man that loves his moms
i can't trust a mom who has all sons
because i am a woman too
and i know the things we'd do
to survive

BAD FARMER

i know her as the seed destroyer
i knew the bottom of her shoe
more than i knew the sun from God

INT. GRANDFATHER RHODES HOUSE

BEGIN FLASHBACK: BREE visited her GRANDFATHER
RHODES when she was younger. And she may have
found out why some men acted a certain way. DAD
told her GRANDFATHER used to sleep on his roof
at night back in the day. I think to myself oh
wow what a dream. Counting the stars, making
wishes, and watching the clouds move in the
dark. No, DAD said GRANDFATHER had to watch the
families back. Sometimes the KKK would come
through raging and tormenting Blacks so he
slept with the rifle slung over his back. My
Grandparents lived on a farm which was safer
because some white bosses in the suburbs would
drive to their employees' neighborhoods and
call out their wives or daughters. And the
Black men had to send them out and they'd drive
them away and then bring them back. If they
didn't obey they would have lost their good
paying jobs. FLASHBACK ENDS

EUPHEMISM

i'd agree with you
but then we'd both be wrong
however my conception
is proof that two wrongs
do make a right
its creepy when you love your abuser
and the advice they give could be good
like the time she said...

HEALING

don't go to a coffee machine expecting tea
don't go to a coffee machine expecting tea
i saw she did not love herself
i should've known she couldn't love me

don't go to a coffee machine expecting tea
don't go to a coffee machine expecting tea
accept the person who's in front of you
don't wish what they could be

when you leave
as hard as it will be
you'll have to find
some sort of responsibility
in all that transpired

it'll keep you out of that victim mentality
it's called taking back your power

don't go to a coffee machine expecting tea
don't go to a coffee machine expecting tea
i saw she did not love herself
i should've known she couldn't love me

many people come here
born because of many different reasons
if you weren't
born from love then repeat after me
don't go to a coffee machine expecting tea
don't go to a coffee machine expecting tea

because God has everything we need

DON'T GO

out into the world a birl
a birl is a
b l a c k   g i r l
with a black mother
who didn't teach her
who she was
or even worse
whose she was

INT. ROSWELL HIGH SCHOOL / after school
activities

CAST ME AS PRINCESS

my mama cleaned houses
barely.
she cleaned part of them
and we cleaned the rest
we cleaned on weekends
we'd clean
we'd rest
my father hated us cleaning
especially in white folk houses
he said too many people died
for us to be washing they toilet
i think to myself
well apparently not enough
my biggest fear was
walking into a person's house to clean
and realize they go to my school
i remember one house we cleaned
and the woman was my brother's old teacher
you could feel her say
i knew this what you'd be
however
there was one customer
i loved
we called her Ms. Venya
meaning loveable
of hindu origin
and that she was
when we arrived to her house
she gave us tea
she was a stay at home mom

but she went to school
like her husband
with degrees
but because she was pregnant
she was at home
and her husband had her mom
and sister flown from india to join her
to keep her company.
after we cleaned she
cooked us dinner
and the food was so good
it taste like butter
the curry made me smack
and the yogurt
brought me back
IT WASN'T NO LEFTOVERS
everything made by scratch
i watched her pull out
rice straight from the burlap
and i said
to myself
i love indian culture
for caring for their staff
everyone that worked in they house
they treated high caste
they bought us garments and gifts
and gave me memories of my past
like kingdom and royalty
like diamonds that last
all the bad things
i heard bout indians
don't matter to me now
and all the hateful you speak
don't think, bow down
i'm not your subordinate
don't ever tell me my caste

you two steps away from
kissing my ass
then i realized
what a privilege it'd be
to kiss any part of me
the back of my hand
my soul or my feet
so to anyone who
taught me this hate
just know
imma free all people
where black castles await

According to BREE'S Uncle, if her FATHER hadn't
left, none of this would have happened. BREE
says, "if it was already my fate maybe it's good
that he did, maybe his staying would have
altered his kids".

INT. GROCERY STORE / after school activities

BREE remembers being excited to see her DAD to
take her somewhere, anywhere, she liked being
seen out with him to let people know that she
had a DAD. Not everybody has their FATHER and
she believed she was lucky to only see him
sometimes. Kids from her childhood, that she's
spoken to, didn't have one which reminds me

                    BREE

          i wonder where do they go?

        as we're checking out the grocery line
          my dad stops a lady on her way inside
            we in the south were big butts grow
        oohhhh sister you lookin mighty fine,
                    praise the lord
      i was mad cause women hate being cat called
                  they looked at me too
        thinking to themselves, wow in front of his
                      daughter
      i was mad cause my dad never complimented me
        he only tells other women of they beauty
          my mom was right, i really am ugly

            the man gives him our groceries
          my dad hands me the receipt and said
      "when you get older make sure to pay me back,
                    you hear?"
                i was embarrassed
                  i said okay
        besides only pretty girls get free things
                like in the movies

i took the receipt and
stuck it in my pocket
trying not to make eye contact
with the register staff
silly for me to have thought
he did all these things because he liked me
sooner or later i stopped asking for things
because i wasn't sure if i could pay him back
and of course it don't count
the times i had to ask for stuff
just so mom will let me use her phone
"ma can i use your phone,
i need to ask dad for blankadie blank"
or sometimes it was
laughing at her insults
that will get me more minutes
or chime in
how i hate black men
will give me some privacy
and she'll step outside while i talked
when i went to school
i stopped writing my last name
on everything
i was embarrassed of my dad
i began to wonder why are they here
and what do they do?
i faked it so much
i hated men too

i watched the news
when i lived with pastor and first lady
they house was so big
and they had lots of food
a man was being chased by cops and helicopters
and i said "oh God, WHAT DID HE DO?"
apparently his ex wife
took his kids

and wouldn't let him see them
so, he picked her up from school
i thought yeahhh that's what Daddy's do
they fight for they kids
they be all in the news
i wonder why my pops never did
took me to court and ask that i live
my Uncle was a lawyer
why didn't dad ask him for help
you give his boy yo son name
din dont watch yours develop
i wonder why he didn't fight for me
keep us close to his family
why he walked away
why wasn't i enough
"VICTORIA"
what did you say?
usein my government name
like i aint hidden
like ain't not champion
like you don't know me
news flash daddy
i earned the name BREE

INT. ROSWELL HIGH / school activities

BREE

a boulder, an ocean, a friend
they have one thing in common
if you don't watch it carefully
it'll crush you like hard math
it's obvious the division
all the black and hispanic kids
stood in line on one side of the cafeteria
while all the white students were seated
we ate the nasty school lunch
and the white kids all had
monogrammed packed food
i chilled outside
after our debates in class
i think about my nightmares
counting sheep in my sleep
i think about how much
i should assign responsibility
i think about the girl
who asked
"why we celebrate black history"
and i feel my tournament
and anger rising in me
i heard "black people
should be over those things"
and i cry when i dream
and i cry in my sleep
and i cry when they stare
as they cry white tears
as i think about all
the slave beatings i've received
that i think that they see
and i'm scared they don't care
as i think about my mother
and how she raised her heirs

BREE has a memorable moment at kamp kizzy

BREE

we was in the computer lab
doing homework
when ms. word
pointed out
a new summer flier.
there's a camp
happening soon
i think you girls would be interested
it's in your age group
wait what, you said they'll be food
so i signed me and sister up
and packed my purse too
for the most important part
of my entire girlhood
i walked in the door
and met red ruby's love
they call her ms. KESHIA
i call her HEAVEN'S DOVE
i sat in our class
making vision boards grow
i ripped up pages
of black women you know
i glued them down
and she framed it up tight
i thought maybe, just maybe
if i ask God He might
coach SHAYLA said this
is what i will be
i asked *are you sure*
she said *yeah* of course
if it's what i wanted for BREE

we went to lunch
and she announced
us our homework
she said go back home
and write me a poem
or a story of someone

i was interested in this
so i wrote down a poem and
i brought in a lightbulb
that i sculpted to show'em

with it turned upside down
i bent up a hanger
that made it stay
i took out the powder
and wires in the way

i filled it with water
and placed in a flower
when i showed ms. KESHIA
she said
this is your power

i went to our last class
where i cried like a baby
cause the topic was Love
and mothers and hating
coach SHAYLA came to me
and asked me what's wrong
i said nothing,
just nothing, i wanna go home

then she said guess what
i said what is it lady
she said ms. KESHIA
need my help
to read for the finale

i walked in the
auditorium hearing
the girls sing
the camp song
"kamp kizzy
where girls grow
super sweet smart
we walk with a glow"

i walked to the stage
with a block in my throat
i felt cold and dark
outside like mr. Toad
i couldn't speak
nothing came out
i froze, then i melt
i ran down the aisle

i'm back in the classroom
i said that it was stupid
to get up and go speak
i knew i couldn't do it

coach SAHYLA came after me
she said let's try that again
imma go with you this time
i said, okay than

here's my first ever poem
the one coach SHAYLA read
i was so scared
i almost fainted dead

WHEN GIRLS GROW

when a girl grows
she'll start as a seed
soil, sun and water
she'll get what she needs

when a girl grows
she'll develop her roots
to help her stand strong
add in some fertilizer
it'll help her last long

when a girl grows
animals will come to eat her
so she'll need to grow
some thorns and a wax coating
to protect her

and even though
she can make her own food
she'll still need a bit of help
from me and you

BREE needed an escape plan to freedom!

ESCAPE PLAN pt1

you have to at least realize
something is wrong
you have to get to the point where
you can't take it anymore
then choose yourself
get far far away, for a while
so if you come back,
which you might, it's confirmed
the distance brought calm.
try and ask them to treat you better
because there is a God and
people do change.
but be for real right now
you know it'll
take a miracle.
they have to help themselves.
Love is God.
Love is patient, kind, truth, resilient,
faith, hope, endurance, perseverance,
it does not envy, it does not boast,
it is not arrogant, it is not rude,
it is not selfish, it is not anger,
it is not resentment, it does not rejoice in
wrongdoing
if they did not treat you this way
they did not love you
so accept that.
next cry because it hurts, having parents alive
and not in your life.
heal the child inside,
and remember the things you liked to do.
do all those things and more:

draw, paint, ride your bike, color books,
make music, take a hike and climb a tree.
try not to explain yourself to others,
they'll just tell you to forgive them because
EvRyBoDy MaKeS mIsTaKeS.
you eventually will forgive them but it'll take
time
you have to forgive yourself first
and you have to Love yourself first
then next restore your relationship with your
good good Father
you may have to cut others off too,
who report your personal business to that person
you may find yourself a new community
you may have to leave a sibling,
your blueberry muffin.
a day will come where
you can go back for them
or they will come running to you
your pain won't be the worst thing in the world
your pain WILL be understood by someone you
know.
then redefine the lessons you learned
and help your body breath new habits
this continued process of challenging
the bad knowledge and replacing with
the good knowledge
is called spiritual warfare.
so put on the full armor of God
the helmet of salvation, the breastplate of
righteousness, the shield of faith, the belt of
truth, the sword of the spirit and the feet of
peace.
please don't go back, but i know you will
if you're deciding to stay, first test the
spirit

because God may not know them.
look to see if they bear any fruit of the
spirit
Love, joy, peace, forbearance, kindness,
goodness, faithfulness, gentleness and SELF
CONTROL.
before you share with anyone, fill your cup
because it's not selfish
soon enough you'll run into your passion and
purpose
and after reading your bible
you'll realize how many people don't
and after spending time with God
you'll recognize His voice.
find a therapist, save money for your purpose
stay away from narcissists, delete their
contacts
if others don't approve, just know they enjoy
being abused.
write their obituary, don't force no one to
change
cry because it's a painful process.
tell your story to help others, not for
validation
hearing a loved one say they don't believe you
is worse than what you went through
TRUST ME.
to mend her mind, body and soul
BREE stopped eating meat for clearance
BREE is still healing dis ease in her body
BREE watches youtube for information and
understanding of God's word
this can not substitute the reading of the
bible tho
in no specific order BREE listened to

TONY GASKIN
read a woman's influence
RC BLAKES JR
read queenology
DOCTOR RAMANI
PHIL COFER
read *10 easy alkaline smoothies & juices*
YAHKI AWAKENED
SOFT WHITE UNDERBELLY
JAY SHETTY PODCAST
FAITH & FRICTION
CHLOE X HALLE
music & tea time stories
GYPSYJANE6352
hilarious story times too
KNOW FOR SURE PODCAST
MEGAN ASHLEY
KELLY STAMPS
FULLY RAW KRISTINA
GILLIAN BERRY
read e*asy raw vegan recipes*
JUST DIFFERENT
HARDLY INITIATED
DEAR FUTURE WIFEY
PROPHET LOVY

JERRY FLOWERS JR
EMY MOORE
KARAMO SHOW
MICHEAL TODD
THE BASEMENT WITH TIM ROSS
ASHLEY HETHERINGTON
PONTIAC MADE DDG VLOGS
cause watching his family gives me hope
it helps me dream
and believe in black wealth
and also because of HALLE
i llooooove you HALEEEEEEEEE girllllllllll:)
AVA DUVERNAY
PETER SHUB
PRINCESS SARAH CULBERSON
AMANDA GORMAN
RUPI KAUR
WHITNEY HANSON
MALALA YOUSAFZAI
ES DEVLIN
SHONDA RHIMES
ISSA RAE

you have to learn to
eat the meat and spit out the bones
or better yet
take what you need
leave what you don't
use what you learned
and pray bout the unknown
i couldn't get it right on the first try
but trying over and over again
is practice for becoming the person
you're aiming for
and growing into
BREE speaks she is healed,
in presentence
then she ate more fruits than anything
this will aid in dropping bad habits
like unhealthy addictions
for BREE it was sugar specifically
please don't be silly you know
white sugar is not the same sugar that exist in
fruit
and she stayed away from drinking milk
that was the biggest Love move she made
once you can Love your enemy, and treat them
like they aint done anything wrong to you
that's how you know you've died and been reborn
when you make it out
just remember
to breathe

now you're ready to escape.
just let go

and let God.   ☻

FLASHFORWARD: See Me Human

EXT. GEORGIA SOUTHERN UNIVERSITY aka original
GSU - DAY
BREE arrived freshman semester on campus Summer
of 2014, she finally gets a taste of freedom. On
her way to the cafeteria with her two friends
she sees a truck is driving by full of frat boys
from down the street. I don't need to tell you
what color they is, only what they said to me.
"Niggers!" I did what any black person would
have. I kept walking to my destination just
faster. I cried myself to sleep that night
thinking only ignorant people were supposed to
behave like that, I thought to myself only
isolated country folk were supposed to think
like that. We here are a new generation, we
trying to become doctors, lawyers and teachers.
No way this is a willing choice, no way this is
real still this day. I was so naive, I was so
BREE.

SEE ME HUMAN

HARBIN was my first puppy i trained
for 16 months
confidence, socialization, security
those were my instructions to a successful
service animal
black was his coat
black was his soap
his cute black paws
when they stopped to look at him
a dog he was called
i told everyone yes
he is allowed in here and yes
anything with a mouth can bite and yes
i am his mama
i often said no
we will not move and no
here's what you not gonna do and no
he is not for sale
he learned every second of the day
annoyed cause they'd touch him unafraid
everywhere i go, he went
everything he learned, i didn't
him black them blue
you sit
you stay
or i'll shoot
dogs were better raised, who knew
seeing and knowing that i wasn't
angered that this was how i found out
how to be human
just
don't
bark.